Dedicated to my husband Justin, and children Jacob and Jocelyn

Copyright © 2021 Jennifer Kaufman
All rights reserved.

It Seems to Me That You Can Be

By Jennifer Kaufman

Illustrated by Heather Workman

You can be a...

Teacher

You can be a...

Pilot

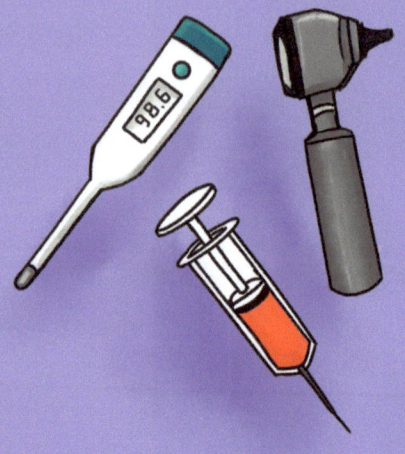
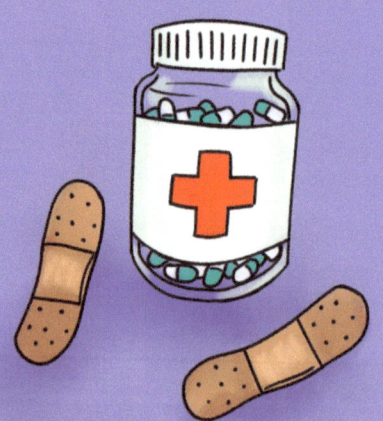

You can be a...

Doctor

You can be a...

Plumber

You can be a...

Chef

You can be an...

Electrician

You can be a...

Police Officer

You can be a...

Veterinarian

You can be a...

Flight Attendant

You can be a...

Firefighter

You can be a...

Bus Driver

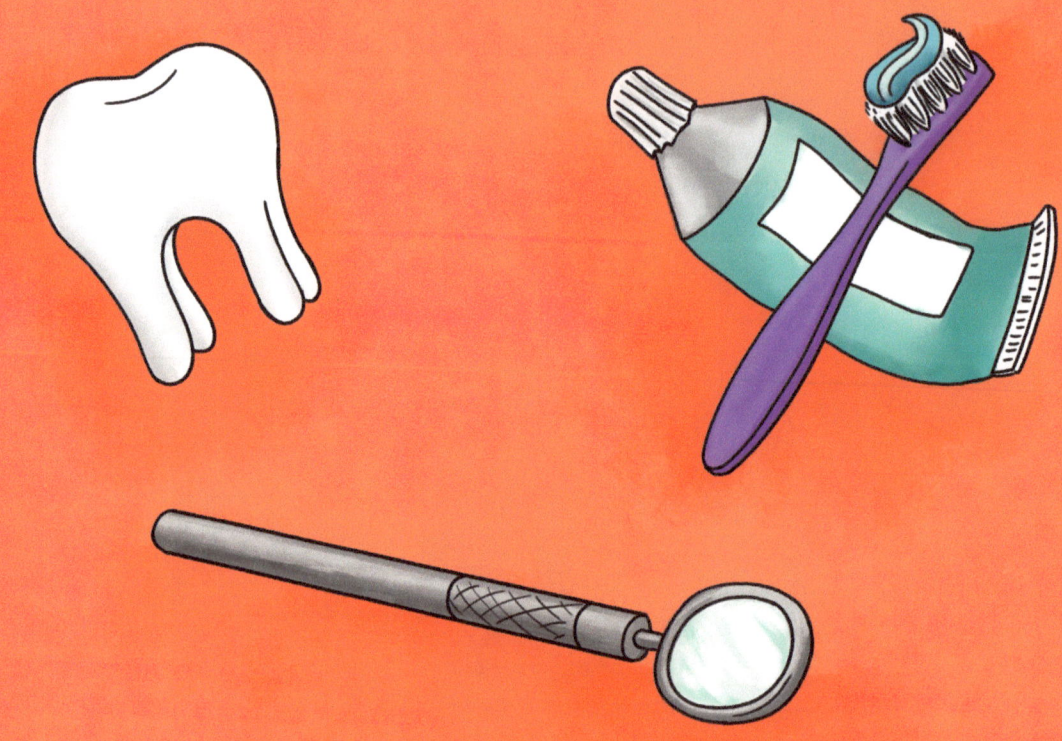

You can be a...

Dentist

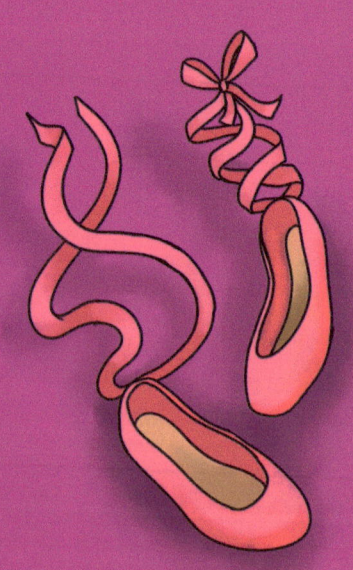

You can be a...

Dancer

It seems to me you can be anything you want to be...

As long as you are **happy!**

www.ingramcontent.com/pod-product-compliance
Lightning Source LLC
Chambersburg PA
CBHW041200290426
44109CB00002B/86